POEMS

OF

PRAISE

FOR

HIS GLORY

Missionary Shirley Dennis Richards

TABLE OF CONTENTS

Shirley L. Dennis's
book

Stories jokes poems

Songs pictures etc.

INTRODUCTION

Thank God for dedicated teachers who instill a love and appreciation for "some of the better things in life." As a student in the Los Angeles Unified School District, I was blessed with many wonderful teachers.

In the second and third grades we were asked to write poems or other expressions. That was the beginning of my love affair with writing. At the age of "almost 80" I enjoy reading my first self-published book from third grade. My love for writing has increased over the years, especially in my retired years. As of this date, my autobiography "GO TO AFRICA? WHO? NOT ME!" is scheduled to be published within weeks.

My interest in traveling was implanted by my third grade teacher. She probably had no idea that one of her students would someday travel to Mexico, Central America, South America, Caribbean, Europe, Africa and Canada. Living in the ghetto was NO HINDRANCE to my dreams.

How blessed my life has been (and continues to be). My two talented granddaughters, Celeste (college student) and Colette (middle school student), have both shown talents in writing skills.

I praise God for all of His numerous blessings to me.

Mrs. Shirley L. Richards

DEDICATION

This book is dedicated to several outstanding persons in my life:

- Jesus Christ is at the top of the list because He transformed my life and gave me the gift of writing.

Friends and family come next:

- Cousin Yolanda Bozant, a published writer and one of the smartest people I know, for her help and encouragement of ALL of my writings.
- Grand-daughters Celeste and Colette who give me inspiration to write.
- Anointed cousin, Angel Deshotel, who wrote: "I am 12 years old and a nine-year brain cancer survivor. Writing is my life. All of my life I have prayed to have a published book". She has two books already.
- Helen Jacobs and Ethelyn Taylor, who have encouraged me for years to have my poetry published.
- Birma Castle, president of the Beaumont Poetry Society, who inspires us at each of our local meetings. This octogenarian, abounds with energy and enthusiasm for poetry, which is contagious.
- My Good Friend Lovely Brown, who taught in Watts, California for her entire career, turning down positions at elite schools.
- And all the teachers who are teachers indeed. God Bless Them!

From **PROSPERITY**
to **POVERTY**
to **POWER**

Habakkuk 3:17, 18
*"Although the fig tree shall not blossom, neither shall fruit
be in the vines; the labor of the olive shall fail,
and the fields shall yield no meat; the flock shall be
cut off from the fold, and there shall be no herd in the stalls:
yet I will rejoice in the Lord, I will joy in the God of my salvation."*

The fig trees are blossoming
There is much fruit on the vine
My storehouse is filled to capacity
With food of every kind

The supply of olive oil is abundant
A bumper crop has come from the field
Most of us are overweight
We have not missed a break, a snack nor a meal.

The flock is flourishing in the fold
And the herd has outgrown the stalls.
It is obvious that we need larger quarters
We'll expand and break out these walls.

Wait! A catastrophe has occurred
And all that was owned is gone
There is not a chicken in every pot
There isn't even a dry soup bone.

Is it time to cry out?
Is it time to weep and moan?
Is it time to think of suicide?
Or is it time to seek recluse and be alone with Him.

Lord, you have freely given
And it is yours to take away,
You are the giver of the night
As well as the giver of the day.

For a time my heart was heavy
Burning tears came to my eyes
Questions and doubts tormented me
With an unending list of whys.

Then your peace enveloped me
and your joy flooded my soul
My broken pieces came back together
Like parts of a puzzle you made me whole.

My circumstances are the same
But the change had been made within
My confidence in you is even greater
I can trust you no matter how, why or when.

SLR ~

SET FREE

Zechariah 3:1-5

I am a brand plucked out of the free. Hallelujah!
I am His chosen vessel. Praise the Lord!
I am in unity with the Godhead.
We are on one accord.

My filthy garments have been removed. Hallelujah!
A fair *mitre* (clean turban) has been placed on my head.
I have been miraculously cleansed and set free
By the One who came, suffered, was crucified
and rose again from the dead.

Satan, you came to condemn me
But you were stopped in your tracks.
Jesus, my advocate, stood between us.
You were forced to retreat and get back.

Satan, you've been defeated! Hallelujah!
You no longer have power over me.
Jesus conquered you on Calvary
And made it possible for me to be set free.

Free! Free! I have been set free!
I shout it for all to hear
"Set free for how long?" The question might be asked,
Not for just a day, a month or a year...but for all eternity.

Hallelujah! Jesus has set me free!!

SLR ~

SICK

Dedicated to Sis. Ruth Harris

Lord, I have been sick so long
And I wonder if I will ever get well
I ask to be healed for Your glory
That your message I may continually tell.

You've allowed many lives
My pathway to cross
You've allowed me to be a light
And a guide to the lost.

There were years as an office worker
When I strove to uplift Your name
It was common knowledge that I was a Christian
Of You and Your name I was not ashamed.

How I enjoyed serving you at Pilgrim
In every capacity I could
As a Sister I respected my place
I didn't try to boss the preacher nor the brotherhood.

Mine was to encourage
And I did my very best
It wasn't always easy
But I'm sure I passed the test.

Lord, you still perform miracles
Because you have done many in my life.
I have seen you remove dark clouds,
Envy, sarcasm and strife.

Just as you removed these
You can remove cancer from this body of mine.
Do with me as you please.
My body, my life, my soul are thine.

My hope is here in this life
But the greatest is yet to come some day
I can live to be 50, 90, or 100
You, Lord, have the final say.

Whatever length of days are mine
In whatever physical condition I might be
I can have joy, peace and assurance
Because I know that you love me.

Someday I'll stand before you
And see your face in peace.

Hallelujah!

SLR ~

ASKING FOR MONEY

Asking for money isn't easy
But the Cause justifies the means
Especially if those for whom it is raised
Have suffered, sacrificed, and on others have to lean.

Some of our pockets are deep
And the contents in abundance are packed
While some pockets are shallow
With many of life's luxurious lacked.

However, the same call
Comes to rich, middle class and poor alike
Give! Give to God's service
Don't withhold or boycott or go on strike.

There are those who are sacrificing
Their time, their talent, their all
To spread the love of Jesus
And encourage mankind upon His name to call.

How much should be given?
And to which needy cause?
So many voices are clamoring
And our gift can seem so small.

Ask God. He will give direction
And direct which way your money should go
Give to help his workers
Someday you might be the one He will instruct to "Go!"

So, give until God tells you to stop.

SLR ~

RESTORATION

*"and I will restore to you the years that the locust hath eaten, the
cankerworm, and the caterpillar, and the palmerworm,
my great arm which I sent among you."* Joel 2:25

Lord, you sent adversity
And it came in like a flood
Heart ache and misery abounded
There was even shedding of blood.

The locust flew in
And quickly began to destroy
Swiftly all was gone
There was left not even a broken toy.

The cankerworm caused havoc,
Destruction and distress
Out of orderliness came confusion
Everything seemed to be in a mess.

The caterpillar crawled into
Secret places to destroy
Into homes. Into marriages.
Into friendships. Misery to employ.

The palmerworm was the scavenger
Who came to destroy from within
With it came feelings of defeat, frustration, depression
And the inclination to yield to sin.

"Blow the trumpet in Zion,
Sanctify a fast."
Let's go to God for the solution
Hurry! Let's do it fast.
Rend your heart, and not your garments,
And turn unto the Lord your God."
Hallelujah! God in His tender mercy
Has replied to this lump of sod.

Weeping and repentance are in order
From the greatest to the least of all
Self-righteousness and intolerance have been prevalent
This always leads to a fall.

Our church services have become routine
As through the motions we go.
But as far as the fruits of the Spirit are concerned
Very little of this do we show.

We are hard
And abrasive to each other.
We often act as opposing warriors
Rather than as a Sister or Brother.

Lord, we have searched the camp
And You've revealed the cause of our woe
Strange as it may seem, You sent these calamities
Because You love us so.

You have reminded us to put You first
In every area of our life
Then you will enable us to be peacemakers
Rather than makers of confusion and strife.

Lord, you have restored that which was taken away
I will continue to extol your praises until my dying day.

"Be glad then, ye children of Zion,
And rejoice in the Lord your God." (2:23)
He is dealing with us in love and mercy
And not with a chastening rod.

SLR ~

FEAR

PSALM 56
David fled from Saul in fear for his life.
In Gath, the city to which he had fled, he feared again because his
fame as a warrior was well known.

He pretended to be insane so that the Philistine king
would not consider him to be a threat.
I Samuel 21:10-11

Lord, I am a mere mortal
And I fear for my life
I ran from my home in terror
Leaving all – my comforts, friends, children and even my wife.

I am being hunted like an animal
On the run day and night
Peace seems to elude me
Those I meet seem bent on a fight.

I've had to demean myself
Even pretending to have gone mad
My body was not bathed, my hair not combed
I was almost naked – scantily clad.

Fear was my diet
Morning, noon and night
I jumped at my shadow
And feared every man in sight.

The fear is still here
And conditions have not changed at all.
However, I seem to be highly elevated above them
With no fear that I might fall.

Your words of hope came to mind
And I realized that You were there
Just waiting for me to trust you
And to bring to you my every care.

I ran into your loving, outstretched arms
Crying, "Lord, hide thou me!"
For "What time I am afraid,
I will trust in thee."

Lord, I will praise you.
I will praise you as long as I have breath.
I will praise you in this life
And by your grace, I desire to praise you in death.

SLR ~

I WILL NOT FEAR MANKIND
Psalm 56:4

"I will not fear what flesh can do unto me."
I will not fear on the land, the sea, the air,
    nor wherever I may be.

I will not fear wars, riots, famine nor threats on my life
I will not fear hatred, Jealousy, envy nor strife.

I will not fear living though at times it can be trying to me
I certainly will not fear death because that is
    the doorway to Thee.

So mankind can continually sow havoc
    Throughout the universe
He seems so confused and mixed up
    that he is going in reverse

So why should I fear mortal man, whose breath
    is in God's hand?
I will fear and love the Crucified Lord and for Him
    continue to stand.

Lord I love you!

Lord, I thank you that you first loved me!

Lord Jesus, I thank you for giving me your peace
    that passeth all understanding.

Savior, I thank you because you will come again to get me and I shall
dwell with you throughout eternity.

I praise you, Lord!

SLR ~

HANNAH

MY NAME IS HANNAH, THE WIFE OF ELKANAH.

My husband made a boo boo ...
Instead of having one wife he had two.

AND YOU KNOW THAT ALWAYS SPELLS TROUBLE!

Peninnah – that was the other woman's name ...
She was so fruitful and had children galore.
She taunted me cruelly because I had none...
While the number of hers increased more and more.

WHAT A MISERABLE PREDICAMENT I WAS IN!

Elkanah was a loving husband
Who openly expressed his great love for me
Yet, inside I felt lonely, depressed and self pity
Would not allow me to contented be.

I lost my appetite ....
My health began to fail
My condition was becoming deplorable ...
It was obvious to see – I didn't have to tell.

My husband uttered words of encouragement
That helped to bring me out of my grief
I began to realize the forces of evil
Had robbed me of my joy. THE THIEF!!

I went into the temple
And poured out my hear to the Lord
"HELP ME! HELP ME!" I cried,
"The burden is too hard."

ELI, the priest misunderstood ...
He thought me to be a drunk although it was early in the day
"NO! NO!" I told him, "I am burdened
AND HAVE TO PRAY!"

I am praying, "Lord, give me a man child.
Take away my reproach, I pray.
I'll surely give him back to you
To serve you until his dying day."

"Go in peace," said Eli,
"and may God grant you for that which you ask."
I left there feeling lighthearted and joyful within ...
God's peace had shined down upon me and in it I did bask.

AND TIME MARCHED ON ....

HALLELUJAH!! THANK YOU GOD
FOR HAVNG MERCY ON ME!!
THANK YOU FOR ANSWERING PRAYER... THANK YOU
FOR THIS PRECIOUS GIFT WHICH I NOW SEE!!!

YOU HAVE GIVEN ME A MAN CHILD ...
JUST AS I REQUESTED IN MY PRAYER.
A little one who is precious and helpless ...
And who will need my tender, loving care.

I will love him ... I will cherish him ...
I will faithfully train him too.
Then when he is weaned I WILL FULFILL MY VOW ...
AND GIVE HIM BACK TO YOU.

As a small child he was weaned ...
He was taken to serve under Eli the priest.
"Bless you for keeping your vow, my daughter," he stated,
"and may your family continue to increase!

PRAISE THE LORD!
HE HAS ANSWERED PRAYER AGAIN!
Three more sons and two daughters now are mine.
Thank you Lord for being so faithful, so generous and so kind!

I VOW ANOTHER VOW:
TO SERVE YOU, LORD, UNTIL I DIE.

SLR ~

MY TEARS

Psalm 56:8

Put thou my tears into thy bottle, Lord.
You know why each one was shed.
Some were for Saints enduring hard places in life
Many were for backsliders who were deceived and misled.

I remember tears I shed as I prayed for
Loved ones that were sick.
Some were healed. Some died.
It was you who made the pick.

Lord, I can't help but laugh as I think of
The foolish tears I shed for what I did not need.
I would come to you in childish ways
And I would beg and plead.

You let me cry, you let me squirm,
Until I finally accepted your will.
You knew all along what was best for me.
I could only see in the valley,
You knew what was over the hill.

Tears of disappointment were shed
Because many times my feelings were hurt
Later it made sense to realize that I needed to be stronger
I needed to be more alert.

Wayward children and mates
Also caused the tears to fall
The seeming impossibility of the situation
Made me feel as helpless as an animal in a stall.

Financial worries often caused
Me to have misty eyes
Sometimes you answered quickly, sometimes seemingly slow
In whatever length of time, you always heard my cries.

Tears were shed for those who are lost
And on their way to hell
For them the tears continually flow
As from a deep dug well.

Lord, save all these tears
And keep them there for me
They will be another reminder of your love and concern
Throughout all eternity.

SLR ~

DEAR NUMBER TWO

Dear Number Two
I was thinking of you today
And thought of writing and asking, "How are you?"

Daily you are in my thoughts and in my prayers too
You are a wonderful, kind and loving son
And I want to remind you how much we love you.

The miles separate us although we do talk by phone
Many times we get lonesome for you
But rejoice to know you are not alone.

Aiding within you is the Father, Son and the Holy Ghost
We rejoice to hear how you are reading your bible,
Praying and yielding to the Heavenly Host.

All in your life is not perfect nor will it ever be
Yet, we have the hope that someday your household
Will increase from one … to two … to three …

God answers prayers. We can all testify to this.
He sees every tear. He hears every prayer.
Not a one will He miss.

Isn't it wonderful that we can serve Him
And stay in touch with Him every day?
As we realize our dependence upon Him
We continue to acknowledge Him
And allow Him to direct our way.

SLR ~

ACCEPTED IN THE BELOVED
Ephesians 1

I am accepted in the beloved.
I am born again from above.
Hallelujah!

I am adopted into God's family
He has given me a royal pedigree
Praise the Lord!

I am redeemed through His blood
My sins are washed as I stand under its flood.
Glory!

Wisdom and prudence are mine for the asking
I am saved! Saved! Saved! In this realization I am basking.
Thank you, Jesus!

The Holy Spirit has put His seal upon me.
I am no longer Satan's slave. I have been set free.
Hallelujah!

I have the power within to dwell in this filthy world.
And keep my garment white though garbage at me is hurled.
Praise the Lord!

I can look temptation in the eye and call the devil a lie
I can endure hard places in life and never whimper or cry.
Glory!

All this power is mine because of what Jesus did for me.
I'm going to let my light shine. I'll be bold for Him.
	He has set me free!

Thank you Jesus!

SLR ~

I HAVE STRUCK IT RICH

I am rich! Rich! Rich!
At last I've struck it rich!

I now have more than I'll ever need.
No longer will I have to borrow, beg or plead.
Wow! I'm really rich!

I can now buy all that my heart could desire
Now I can get the luxuries and necessities
      that this life does not require.

I'm not poor anymore!

Let me get my hat and coat. I am going to shop galore.
I don't have to penny pinch because there is always more.
Right on!

My list is long and my baskets will be loaded
I am going to enjoy this and nothing will be corroded.

First I'll get some grace, and then lots of love.
A double portion of understanding and hope from above.

I also need: faith, peace, longsuffering, patience, joy, wisdom,
gentleness, goodness, faith, meekness, temperance

And my list goes on and on. I can get more and more.
Shopping is fun. No money is needed in the
      Heavenly Department Store.
Come and join me. Help yourself to all.

SLR ~

IN THE SHADOW OF THY WINGS
Psalm 57:1

*"In the shadow of thy wings will I make my refuge,
until these calamities be overpast."*

In the shadow of thy wings I had sought refuge
From the raging storms of life.
I had turned to your Word for guidance
I needed Divine revelation, not human advice.

With arms outstretched you took me in,
You coddled and comforted as a mother hen would her chicks
You shielded me from the blows of this life:
From the hatred, strife, misunderstandings and verbal licks.

After the comforting was over
And after the tears were dry
You sent me back out to face the world
With tenderness you encouraged me to give it a try.

With halting steps and trembling knees
I went out to face the giants of life.
Like David, I had my sword of faith
I was to be a warrior, not a human sacrifice.

Then the Spirit energized me
And I heard, "Let the weak say I am strong."
God stood me up in boldness and strength
He filled me with peace and joy. He put in my heart a song.

"I am the victor in Jesus," I shouted.
I said it for all to hear.
Fear of life has succumbed to assurance
Because the Savior is near – with me – right now!

SLR ~

MY BEAUTIFUL BLACK CHILD

You are beautiful
    With your smooth bronze skin
You are beautiful
    With your tight kinky hair.

You have been told that your lips are think
            and
That your nose is big

Were you also told that these are your distinctive marks of beauty?

From the crown of your head
            to
The tip of your toes,
You are a beautiful Child!

Your athletically strong body
            and
Your sharp analytical mind
Enhance your beauty, my child.

Just let me look at you.
My, my, what a wonderful sight you are to behold!
I love you! I am proud of you!
I am thankful to God that you are
    MY BEAUTIFUL BLACK CHILD!

SLR ~

GIVE US SOUL MUSIC

Give us music for the Soul
The flesh is already over fed
Give us lyrics that have meaning
Rather than extra loud beats instead.

Why all the insistence on noise,
When the Lord can come in a quiet still voice?
Our souls need spiritual food.
There is no other choice.

Lord, it seems as though the music
Is becoming more important than the preached Word.
Many seem to shun "thus saith the Lord,"
They leave church thinking of only the music they have heard.

Lord, help us to get the right perspective
To put things in their proper place
For spiritual food give us a desire
Bur for flesh satisfiers, cause us to lose the taste.

Enable us to enjoy good music
But not put the main emphasis there.
Your preached Word is where the power lies
That is the message we are to share –
                                    With the world.

SLR ~

MY HIDING PLACE

"Thou art my hiding place;
thou shalt preserve me from trouble…." (Psalm 32:7)

We all need a hiding place from:

- The storms of life
- The disappointments that could destroy us
- The illnesses that befall us
- The misunderstandings that hurt us
- The sins that weaken us
- The trials that test us
- The harsh words that chaff us
- The loneliness that haunts us
- The busyness that drains us
- The flood of sin that is rampant today
- The bleak outlook of our nation – and our world.

Hallelujah!!

Thank God we do have a hiding place!

"…Thou shalt compass me about with songs of deliverance."

SLR ~

LOSTNESS
Luke 15:11-24

Law of diminishing returns:
The more a person tries to gratify fleshly appetites and desires, the less satisfaction is gained.

Mankind is lost in:
> The killing race for progress
> The runaway race for status
> The sensuous thirst for sex
> The degrading desire for drugs
> The pompous desire for popularity
> The maddening desire for money
> The aching desire for acceptance
> The flood of passion and pleasure seeking.

Waiting for us in the Father's house is:
> Food for the hungry
> Friends and companionship for the lonely
> Meaning and purpose for the discouraged
> Self-esteem for the downtrodden
> Riches for the poor
> Water for the thirsty
> Joy for those in sorrow
> Peace for the troubled
> Salvation for the repentant sinner.

SLR ~

SEARCHING
Psalm 25

"Remember not the sins of my youth, nor my transgressions...."
(verse 7)

Lonely, longing for love
Menacing, mind boggling need for money
Depths, darkness, and depression of despair
Seemingly sensible but seductive desires of sex.

Belittling burden of being bedridden
The sad, soul searching times of sickness.
The teeming, tumultuous times of trouble.

Lessons learned from the three un's -
    1) Un-loved   2) Un-appreciated 3) Un-wanted

Add to that the two mis –
    1) Mis-understood 2) Mis-placed

A few nots add the icing to the cake:
    1) Not seen   2) Not heard   3) Not sought for

After these have been experienced, we are better equipped to do the work of God.

SLR ~

GOD CAN
Psalm 27

God can make the high places become low:

Hard	Easy
Crooked	Straight
Steep	Level
Dark	Light
Slippery	Firm

God can be a friend to the friendless:

Shelter	Homeless
Physician	Sick
Bread	Hungry
Water	Thirsty
Comfort	Heartbroken
Rest	Weary
Sight	Blind
Joy	Sorrowing
Riches	Penniless pauper

SLR ~

I HATE SIN!
Psalm 51

"I acknowledge my transgression…" (Psalm 32:5)

I HATE SIN!
Especially when it's in me.

I HATE SIN!
Because it crushes, enslaves and never sets free.

I HATE SIN!
It causes such misery and pain.

I HATE SIN!
It hides the light of the sun and only lets me see rain.

I HATE SIN!
It makes me mistreat you
And I forget that you are human
And have your faults too.

Most of all I HATE SIN
Because it separates me from God.

THANK GOD FOR JESUS, OUR "SIN BEARER."

SLR ~

HATED WITHOUT A CAUSE
Psalm 54

Saul, David's father-in-law, hated him without a cause. He pursued David to kill him. David and his men often hid in rocks and caves in the wilderness to prevent being discovered by Saul.

On at least two occasions the Ziphites came and told Saul that David was hiding in their land.

Strangers and oppressors search to destroy me
They seek after my soul
No wrong have I done unto them
Why, Lord, are they so bold?

My face they have never beheld
They would not know me by sight
Yet they hate me with a hatred so intense.
Their hearts are filled with evil – not knowing wrong from right.

I am innocent of any fault
Of which I might be accused
My desire is only to please you, Lord
So evil temptations I have refused.

I thank you for your deliverance
It is already on the way.
Vengeance is yours you have reminded me.
You will repay one day.

With a trusting and rejoicing heart, I await that day.

SLR ~

PRESSURES! PRESSURES!
Psalm 55

It is bad enough to be hurt and betrayed by an enemy but it is even worse when it comes from a close and trusted friend.

Ahithopel had been David's counselor and now he has joined Absalom, David's son who sought to kill hik.. (II Samuel 15:12; Psalm 41:9)

Pressures! Pressures are mounting
They take the joy out of life.
Pressures that come from within and without.
Pressures from envy. Pressures from jealousy
   and pressures from strife.

Sometimes they come in so strongly
And overwhelm me like a flood.
Pressures that seem to drain me of energy,
Of peace, and even life sustaining blood.

If I sprouted wings like a dove
And could fly away and be at rest
It would be my luck to alight in Paradise
And have waiting for me a demanding, worrisome pest.

To wander far off and remain in the wilderness
Isn't the answer, Is it Lord?
The wilderness is awfully barren
And the ground is too hard.

From the windy storm and the tempest
There seems to be no relief.
"I've been robbed!! I've been stripped!
Stop! Stop thief."

"Cast thy burden upon the Lord,
And He shall sustain thee."
Lord, is that promise just for others
Or does it also include me?

Do you really care about the pressures
That haunt me day by day?
Is it because I am not walking your pathway?
Not going your way?

I know you love me
And in my heart you abide.
But sometimes life is like a roller coaster
And I am on a fast ride.

Am I the problem, Lord?
Has self gotten in the way?
You say I need more time in your Word.
I need more time to pray.

You say you sent these pressures.
But Lord, why me? I'm your child.
Yes, I **can** trust you through difficulties.
I **can** continue to witness. I **can** continue to smile.

Evening, and morning, and at noon,
I will pray and cry aloud.
I have found the key to victory!
Prayer relieves pressures and dispels dark clouds.

Lord, please continue to hold my hand
As I cling tenaciously to you.
With you I'm on the winning team.
As I trust, you will bring me through.

SLR ~

A TRAVELER'S GUIDE TO HEAVEN
John 14:2-3

A traveler's guide to Heaven
Is available free of charge
Transportation in First Class
With accommodations that are rich, plush and large.

However, storms will be encountered
As we travel to this distant land.
Neither friend nor foe can stop us
We're safe in the Master's Hand.

Hallelujah! I shout because I'm a traveler
Rejoicing as I go
Jesus has paid for my ticket
I am secure in Him I know.

Written for Women's Day at Pilgrim, L.A.
SLR ~

WHERE IS A RIGHTEOUS JUDGE?
Psalm 58

Justice or injustice - Which should it be?
Injustice for you but mercy and justice for me.

Perhaps you are poor - penniless, without a dime.
Therefore you will have to suffer the severest
   penalty for your crime.

But me, I can slip a bribe and the judge will set me free
Legislators I know can help me; they can pass a new decree.

I'm feeling proud. Although guilty, I am free as a bird.
Your cries and those of others came too
       but I closed my ears pretending I never heard.

What lawyer is this that you foolishly
       claim will plead your case?
I say he can be bribed, be brought --
       if he is a member of the human race.

Your lawyer, you say, never loses and charges no price!
Your lawyer is who? Oh! The Lord, Jesus Christ!

Please introduce me to your lawyer - judge.
I will need him to defend me when I stand before God.

SLR ~

DEFEATED IN BATTLE
Psalm 60

Our enemies have overpowered us
And we have been defeated
It is not the first time this has happened;
History seems to be repeated.

We fought valiantly -
With all our strength and might
The battle raged all day, all evening,
And continued late into the night.

The fighting became exceedingly fierce -
And we were put to flight.
Our hearts were filled with sorrow,
With remorse, and with fright.

"Let's take inventory of ourselves,"
Seemed to be the common thought.
A cause for our dilemma
And the remedy was what we sought.

Slowly the pieces of the puzzle
Began to fit into place.
We had gone into battle presumptuously,
Self-confidently and in haste.

Time had not been taken
To seek God on our knees.
Is it any wonder then that
He failed to hear our pleas?

Unconfessed sins were a barrier
That helped cause our defeat
Not only did it allow enemies to beat us --
But to devour us as raw meat.

Lord, we **praise you** for this difficult lesson
That we have been taught.
Victory comes through trusting you, confessing sins,
Seeking your guidance and rejoicing in the salvation
    you bought --
        With your precious blood.

Thank you for being the **Master-Teacher**.
We have learned our lesson well.

SLR ~

A REVEALER OF SECRETS

Daniel 2:27-30

A revealer of secrets is my God,
Who reigns on the Heavenly Throne.
No matter is too difficult, nor anything hid from Him.
His mighty power is vested in Himself alone.

He reveals secrets
And makes known what shall come to pass.
He knows the end from the beginning.
He knows from the first to the last.

With all this matchless power
And wisdom that we mortals cannot comprehend,
I marvel at His great love and concern
For the wicked children of men.

His love and His mercy flow
Wider and deeper than any earthly river.
Just dwelling on His majesty, His power, and His love.
Reassures me again and again; He is not a taker but a giver.

Lord, you know the secrets
Tucked away, hid and locked in my heart.
I willingly surrender the keys into your hands.
Take out all that doesn't glorify you -- remove every part.

Wash me; cleanse me; Make me pure within.
I want to be used for your glory --
Without spot - Without wrinkle - Without sin.

SLR ~

LORD, I PRAISE YOU

Lord, I praise you
  By the raising and clapping of my hands.
I praise you even more
  By walking uprightly through this land.

I praise you
  By voicing the words when with the congregation I stood
I praise you even more
  By showing love and compassion to my fellow man.

I praise you when I'm with the crowd
  But it is better to praise you when I'm by myself.
I can even praise you quietly;
  You are not hard of hearing; neither are you deaf.

I praise you
  For giving me a thirst for your Word.
I praise you
  For every prayer of mine that you heard.

Lord, I love you
  and
I just want to thank and praise you.

SLR ~

ONLY HE
Psalm 62

Only He has been the strength needed
  When we are weakest
Only He has been our joy during times of sorrow
Only He has been our friend when we were lonely.

Only He has been our bread when we were hungry.
Only He has been our water when we were thirsty.
Only He has been our pathway through the wilderness.

Only He has been our home when we were homeless.
Only He has been our doctor when we were sick.
Only He has been our lawyer when
  we needed defending.

Only He has been our Rock when we stood on
  Sinking sand.
Only He has been our shelter from the storms of this life.
Only He has been our currency when we
  Didn't have a dime.

Only He has been our substitute on the
  Cross of Calvary.
Only He is our Mediator who sits on God's right hand
  To intercede for us.
Only He is our King who will return some day to
  Take us to reign with Him throughout eternity.

SLR ~

SAYING GOODBYE

Saying goodbye is never easy
Even though it has been said time and time again.
A sad feeling tugs at the heart and tears come to the eyes.
Words seem to fail us. We don't know where to begin.

It is hard to think
Of the many miles that will separate us for a while.
But thinking of the day when we will be reunited,
Gives me contentment and causes me to smile.

So instead of "goodbye"
It will be "Until We Meet Again."
My days and nights will be filled with pleasant thoughts
Of you, my very best friend.

SLR ~

HIDING INIQUITY

Thanksgiving After Affliction - Psalm 66

If I regard iniquity in my heart, the Lord will not hear.
Instead of experiencing peace, my life will be troubled
with loneliness, with doubts and with fear.

If I regard iniquity in my heart,
I dwell on the rain rather than on the sunshine in my life.
My thoughts are wrapped up in myself rather than others
And on how I can be a better mother, a better friend, a better wife.

If I regard iniquity in my heart I stray from fellowship in God's Word;
My ears become dull -- It's as though I never heard.

Lord, I confess it! I confess it all to you today!
Please keep me on the narrow path. Never let me stray.

Hallelujah! God has heard me. He has responded to my prayer.
He has never left me. He has always been right there.
But my iniquity had blocked the channel and the
     Blessings couldn't flow.
But Jesus loves and forgives. I know because His Word tells me so.

Blessed be the Lord who hears pray and reserves
     Abundant mercy for all.
This forgiveness is not only mine to claim but it is freely given
     To all who on His name will call.

Lord, we come calling because we need you every day.
We thank you for loving us and hearing us when we pray.
We love -- and adore you and will strive to live in your perfect will
     Because one day we hope to see you face to face
     And to meet you in peace.

UNTIL THEN....
We will keep PRAISING you and TESTIFYING of your love.

SLR ~

I'LL TELL IT
Psalm 67:2; Acts 18:24-28

Yes, I'll tell it
From the rooftops I'll proclaim it.
I'll whisper it softly into the sensitive ears
I'll shout it in the crowd.

Jesus died for sinners!
I'll stand firmly and declare it long and loud.

I'll tell it when I am congratulated
For doing a good job.
Those will also hear it from my lips
Who laugh, ridicule and call me a fool.

Jesus loves the sinner!
All need Him - from those on Knob Hill to those wallowing
   in the slums and cesspools.

I'll proclaim it here. I'll proclaim it there.
Why should anyone not be told?
The message of Jesus must be delivered.
It is more precious than gold.

Jesus intercedes for His children!
This knowledge gives confidence and causes a stand that is bold.

Let's you and I join together and recruit others in this task.
We can speedily spread the message to those who are lost.
Together we can introduce them to the joys of prayer,
witnessing and studying God's Word.
I'll tell them but you can tell them too.
Hurry! The time is short!
   We must reach those who have not heard.

SLR ~

LAURA

Goodbye Laura. Your stay here could have been longer.
Your years could have been extended to 3 score and ten.
But it's too late to dream now
And to think about what could have been.

We were all born into the Morrisey clan
And what a large family were we!
Papa was something else and "did his own thing,"
But Mama taught us and lived before us
   in how a Christian should be.

The years in Durham passed swiftly
And we were thrust into the adult world.
Most of us headed for the big cities.
   I said, "Chicago, here I come!"
Left behind was the slow life -
   tending gardens, feeding chickens and chasing squirrels.

However, you chose to remain in our hometown
You bore one son and later became a registered nurse.
Your skills and abilities allowed you to care for patients
from birth until they were carried away in a hearse.

I don't know where you began to drift
And to get so far off track.
Alcohol seemed more desirable to you than food
Perhaps you drifted so far that you lost the desire to come back.

How I loved you
And longed to see a change in your life!
I prayed for you hundreds of times
It was not just once or twice.

During long distance calls and visits
I would earnestly plead with you.
My exact words were similar to these:
"Laura, Jesus loves you and He died for you too!"

However, we all choose our destinies in this life
You chose yours and I chose mine - they were worlds apart.
But, Laura, you were my sister
And there will always be a place for you in my heart.

Lovely

SLR ~

RELINQUISHMENT

Lord, I relinquish ALL
    I turn the reins over to Your control
        I release to you my life, my family, my home,
            My silver and my gold.

Satan had deceived me
    As he whispered, "Surrender some but not all?
        You don't really have time to read the Bible," he continued,
        "Nor on God's name to call."

"Greater is He that is in me than he that is in the world,"
    This verse came clearly to my mind.
        Thoughts encompassed me of a loving Heavenly Father
            Who is loving, gentle and kind.

My heart overflowed with joy
    As the tears welled up in my eyes
        By God's grace I'll crucify the old nature
            And rejoice as it dies.

Lord, I want nothing between that would separate you and me
    No spot -- No blemish -- No wrinkle -- No sin -- No weight
        I want to love what you love
            And hate what you hate.

Lord, I am nothing within myself

BUT
I REJOICE IN THE KNOWLEDGE THAT I AM YOURS!

H-A-L-L-E-L-U-J-I-A-H!!

SLR ~

LET ME BE A LIGHT

I might not be a Missionary
And travel to some distant land.
I might never leave Los Angeles city limits
But I'll be faithful and do what I can.

I might not be well known
People might not remember my name.
But let my light shine in my community
I don't need to move. My address can remain the same.

I might not be a beauty
Nor dress in the latest style.
Dear Lord, I just want your love to shine through me
As I greet others with kind words and a friendly smile.

I might not have one chick nor child
Then, too, I might have a dozen or more.
Help me, Lord, to gather them and proclaim your wonderful love
Rather than consider them a burden as I shove them out the door.

Dear Lord, I want to be a bright light
I want to shine FOR YOU.

Enable me to be a witness wherever I go
But, most importantly, in my community too.

SLR ~

ANSWERING THE CALL

The call is strong. My heart is troubled.
The missionary call I have heard.
The world so large -- so many lost
Who need to hear God's Word.

But, Lord, I like it here.
It is familiar, comfortable and cozy.
The Salary is good. Relatives and friends are near.
Life is sweet and rosy.

But, Lord, I love you. I truly do,
And I desire to be in your perfect will
But there's a struggle within and often the battle rages.
Show me your way, Lord, step by step. Teach me to yield.

My abilities are limited but I can teach and pray.
As I use my one talent for your glory - you will repay one day.

"Yes, Lord," will be my response when you call me to
    serve you here or there.
"I am your child; I belong to you and will serve you ANYWHERE."

SLR ~

FINDING NEW OCEANS

"New oceans! Wow! Where are they?"
"I can't see them," you say.
Could it be because you got impatient
Because you didn't find them in one day?

In order to find new oceans
You must go further than ankle deep.
It often requires hard study and sacrifice.
Remember that you find that for which you seek.

So, let's set our goals high
Let's aim for the stars.
Let's roll up our sleeves and work hard.
Expecting some hard places, some blows, some scars.

"Nothing ventured, nothing gained.
Is a saying we have often heard.
But believe me, Brothers and Sisters,
It is true - YES, EVERY WORD.

So, let's forget about past failures
Let's forget to keep the score.
Because in order to find new oceans
We must first have the courage to lose sight of the shore.

For Cornelius Taylor

SLR ~

LET THE LIGHT SHINE

Genesis 1:16-18; John 1:6-8

Please let the light shine.
I hate being in the dark.
If not an electric light then a lantern or a candle.
I'll even settle for a spark.

If physical darkness can produce such dread --
Then spiritual darkness must be even worse.
Darkness befell mankind --
It was a part of the curse.

Physical light illuminates
and causes the darkness to flee.
Spiritual light shows me my sin.
The spotlight shines on me.

Lord Jesus, you are my light
And you will show me the way.
Teach me to walk closely with you,
To love and trust you. Teach me to pray.

Sometimes the uphill journey seems too hard to climb.
I become tired, weary, discouraged; I think I might not
        make it at all.
Sometimes the path leads downhill
And I fear I might fall.
Then I remember your Word.
It reminds me you are there and on your name I call.

Hallelujah! Jesus loves me.
And I shall never be alone.
The light of Jesus shining within me
Commands the darkness to be gone.

SLR ~

LONELINESS

Loneliness is hard to bear.
It's no fun to be alone.
It is like dwelling in a dark tunnel
Into which no light has shone.

Loneliness of the body is hard enough to bear
But loneliness of the soul is even worse.
It draws, it drains and causes feelings of despair
It's like living under condemnation -- living under a curse.

But light can shine into darkness
And cause the shadows to disappear.
Sorrow can be replaced by joy
And a smile can erase each tear.

It is not a magic formula
Nor is it sealed with a combination lock.
Jesus offers joy unspeakable
He gives freely to those who will only knock.

SLR ~

DON'T HIDE IT FROM THE CHILDREN
Psalm 78:4

Do not hide it from the children!
Not His Word, nor His praise,
Nor His strength and wondrous works.

Share it with the future leaders
Who will be judges, lawyers, professors,
Nurses, janitors, computer operators, teachers, clerks.

Proclaim it to the little ones
Even before they learn to walk.
Teach them the name of Jesus
As soon as they learn to talk.

Show them His love by your conduct every day.
Be a good witness for Him in thought, word, deed - in every way.

Our inner light needs to shine brightly
So that we not only tell -- but show the way.
That's why we must take time to read the Word,
To meditate, to witness, and to pray.

Jesus loves the children and died that they, too,
Might have eternal life.
They then can face life confidently knowing that
They are prepared to meet Christ -- as His bride -- His wife.

Please, don't hide it from the children!

SLR ~

CALLINGS

Lord, you are the one who calls into missionary service.
There are some you assign to "go" and others are to "stay."
Sometimes your leading seems difficult and hard to understand.
But because of our trust in you, we question - but yet obey.

Materialism and comfort can bind us as a vice.
Our grasp on them can be ever so tight.
Lord, pry our hears away from theses --
You have the might. You have the right.

Help us not to ponder on those who have been assigned to "stay."
Who have not shouldered their share of the load.
The "stayers" often live, eat and drive in luxury
While many of the "goers" often cannot afford to ride
   but must walk the dusty road.

Lord, you are a miracle worker.
You manifest this each day.
Blend us all into one team
To love, to write, to give and to pray.

Lord, may our joint efforts glorify you!

SLR ~

PARENTS IN OLDER AGE

Parents in older age!

Lord, can I laugh as Sarah did?
Not in unbelief, but in sheer delight!

A son to raise TO YOUR GLORY
   TO TEACH of your precepts
   To instruct IN THE WAYS OF RIGHTEOUSNESS
   TO LOVE as you have loved us
   To share OUR HEARTS, OUR HOME, OUR LIVES,
     OUR SUBSTANCE.

He's growing up so fast and seems
   To be betting smarter every day.

Thank you, Lord, for the gifts and abilities
   You have so abundantly bestowed on him.

Thank you most of all for entrusting this priceless
   Privilege to us as .....

     HIS PARENTS.

SLR ~

WE FORSOOK HIM AND FLED

"...Then ALL the disciples forsook Him and fled."
Matthew 26:56

Lord, I'm coming to you in shame today
With a broken heart and a hung down head.
The remorse and turmoil seem too great to bear
It haunts my every waking hour and causes me to
    Toss and turn upon my bed.

Why did I deny you when I swore that I never would?
Why did I falter? Why did I fail?
I am too ashamed to come to you for forgiveness
Does this mean I will go to Hell?

I was afraid of the multitude
Their angry faces frightened me so.
Fear consumed me as I had never experienced before
It went from the top of my head to the tip of my toe.

Lord, is that you calling my name?
Why are you asking if I love you still?
I? Who have so miserably failed?
In shame I confess I love you and still want to do your will.

Lord, why are you loving me so and holding me close to yourself?
Why are you giving me a new charge to "feed your sheep"
Instead of putting me aside on the shelf?

Although I ask why, the answers I already know
You paid the highest price (your blood) that my sins might be
    Remembered no more.
What can I say except 'THANK YOU" for FORGIVING, RESTORING
    And LOVING me so.

SLR ~

PLEASE BE QUIET
(Shut Up)

As I listen to you talk ... and talk ... and talk,
And as I watch you flap your jaws,
I am glad you can't read my thoughts,
Or we would be "at it" with daggers and claws.

Your voice should be worn out,
Because it seldom gets a rest.
You don't permit conversation!
I can't even get in a request!

That tongue of yours must be ready to scream
(I know that is how I feel.)
You work it in overtime.
It never remains still.

It's a wonder it hasn't worn to a frazzle
Or just dropped off from over-use.
You are guilty of a gross crime!
EAR POLLUTION AND TONGUE ABUSE!!

Why am I sitting here
And allowing you to torture me so?
I'll share my little secret.
My body is here but my mind is about to go...go...go!

SLR ~

Ecclesiastes 5:3 and 10:12-14
"...A fool's voice is known by multitude of words."
"The lips of a fool will swallow up himself. The beginning of the
words of his mouth is foolishness: and the end of his talk is
mischievous madness. A fool also is full of his words."

STAND AND TAKE A BOW

Who are you honoring today?
DON'T BE ASHAMED, SHOUT IT LOUD AND CLEAR!
YOU KNOW IT. LET'S SAY IT .....
FATHER'S DAY! FATHER'S DAY IS HERE!!

F is for the friendship we are cultivating each year.
A could be for ADORABLE or ARGUMENTS. We have shared both.
   (Thank God it is not for addict, because we have both
   determined to be drug free.)

T is for THANKFUL, and THOUGHTFUL.
   (Your thoughtfulness had made me thankful that God chose
   You as my dad.)

H is for HEAVEN, both of our final destinations.

E is for ETERNITY that we will enjoy together in God's presence.

R is for RIGHT ON because YOU ARE A SUPER DAD!

                    Signed with LOVE,

                    Your Child

P.S. Dads, you can all stand now and TAKE A BOW!

                                        SLR ~

TRAVELING FEVER

Yes, it's me and I'm off again!
"Where are you going this time?"

Wherever a jet, car, boat or canoe will take me.
I am at peace when traveling. Life is sublime.

Crowded airports . . . . . delayed flights . . . . .
I will take them all.
Traveling! Shopping! Meeting new folk!
Wow! Life is a ball!

I keep my suitcase packed ... just in case
An invitation might come for an ant eating contest
Or a long distance camel race.

I know one day I'll have to slow down
As "Old Rocking Chair" calls my name.

But until then I'm enjoying the wild traveling fever
That never wants to be tamed.

SLR ~

HOW QUICKLY LIFE PASSES

A vapor of smoke - that is what life is like.
And how quickly it flees away.
The hours slip through our fingers like quick silver
And again we behold a new day.

Did I take time to pray?

The months quickly turn into years
And before we know it another decade has passed.
The new shiny things we bought are now old and out of style.
It is hard to find anything dependable that will last and last.

Will I have to suffer for the wrongs I did in the past?

What do I conclude from these rambling thoughts of mine
That causes me to feel uncomfortable - make me squirm?
I don't have all the answers but KNOW God is in control.
On this matter I stand flatfooted and firm.

I am nobody. I myself am just a worm.

So what if life is as a vapor.
Jesus has provided salvation as a gift freely given -- not earned.

Thank you Jesus for the priceless gift!!

SLR ~

ARE WE THAT DIFFERENT?

AWARDED *Honorable Mention* Certificate from
WORLD OF POETRY - 1991

Your dreams may not be my dreams
And your joy might not be the same as mine.

You might be the deep thinking, intellectual type
While I might be the breed of another kind.

Our skin tones may differ
And our mother tongues have a different sound.

My currency may be called dollars, or guilders, or francs
While yours might be called liras, pesos, yens or pounds.

Yet, underneath we are no different -
- You and I.
When cut - we bleed. When hurt - we cry,
When destroyed - we die!

Since we are so much alike -
- You and I

Let's vow to live in peace and harmony
Let's try. Let's really try.

IF NOT,
WE WILL ALL DIE!!

SLR ~

STRIVING FOR GREATNESS

How or who determines greatness?
And how is it best achieved?
By hard work? By pushing and shoving?
Or is it by some strange web we have weaved?

Many search for it ... diligently search
But seemingly to no avail.
Others willingly sell their bodies ... their souls
And march with the crowd ..... **TO HELL!**

"Elevate Yourself!" "Toot Your Own Horn!"
Is the advice from the multitudes of today?
"You deserve to be great, to be honored and admired!"
"Just live your life on credit. You might never have to pay."

To reach the top requires a lot of climbing.
Feet, hands and heads might have to be used for stepping stones.
But if achieving greatness is the driving passion,
Achieve at any cost. Full speed ahead. Let caution be gone.

Ah, greatness! At the top we have finally arrived!
And with a proud look, we stand for the victory pose.
We congratulate ourselves and give ourselves a pat on the back.
Our chest is stuck out, our head held high as we look at others...

.....DOWN OUR NOSE.

But wait, something just is not right.
The crowd is gone, the lights have been turned off
And there is a feeling of fright.

Now, alone in the night with no one to see,
Greatness has paled and reality has set in.
How foolish and deceived we were.
It wasn't greatness and fame we needed ... but it was peace within!

"But seek ye first the Kingdom of God, and his righteousness; and all these *things* shall be added unto *you*."

SLR ~

PSALM 81 (LXXXI)

The people were gathered together in "the solemn day, the day of the feast of the Lord." It was to be joyous.

Why do **people** go to church?
- To be seen or heard?
- To sleep or disrupt?
- To eat or "get something for nothing?"
- To have fellowship and eat spiritual food?
- Because it is a habit and an obligation?

Why do **we** (you and I) go to church?
While we are there, are we worshipping and praising God?
Are we joyful?

Verse 1 - Singing praise to God is a part of our worship to Him. However, some of the songs and music in our churches today sound like LOUD jazz sessions that drown out any vocals. Sometimes it sounds like a competition for fast beats and noise.

Verse 3 - Not only are we to use our vocal chords to praise Him but also musical instruments.

Verse 6 - They were reminded of past blessings. **God** had delivered them from slavery in Egypt; destroyed their enemies and brought them into their own land. We should count our blessings.

Verse 7 - "Waters of Meribah" - Exodus 17:1-7
How often do we murmur and complain about our circumstances? This is not trusting!

Verse 9 - God is jealous of our love and devotion for Him.
He gave us only His very best.
Is it wrong for Him to demand less of us?

Verse 14 - God wanted to abundantly bless His children but their sins prevented Him from doing so.

Is it possible that our disobedience or unconfessed sins is preventing us from enjoying god's best for our lives? If so, let's fall on our knees, beg for forgiveness and then experience His joy and peace that is unsurpassed.

"What can wash away my sins?
Nothing but the blood of Jesus.
What can make me whole again?
Nothing but the blood of Jesus."

Verse 16 - Not only is God concerned about His wayward people, but also with the "haters of God." He is not willing that any should perish.

If God, in all his righteousness, loves sinner, then so should we who are redeemed sinners who have been washed clean by the precious blood of Jesus.

SLR ~

WHO WILL GET THE CREDIT?

Lord, I want to serve you. Yes, I really do!
I want to serve you anywhere and anytime.
I want to be highly respected as a spiritual giant.
But, I wonder, **who will get the credit?**

I know you went to the cross and died for my sins
And I know you sit on the right hand of the Father
And I know you give gifts and callings
Pardon me for asking but **who gets the credit?**

You know I am willing to work and
You know I am not a lazy person
And you know I try to do the best I can
But please, **let me take some of the credit.**

People say I sing good and sound like an angel
They say my sermons are deep and penetrating.
I have been told that I am one of the best Bible teachers around
It's so easy to get a "big head" **and steal some of the credit.**

I try not to be like the publican and
Make it so obvious that I am exalting myself.
I try to look and sound spiritual so that it can't be detected
That this old nature of mine **wants all of the credit!**

You're right, Lord. My biggest problem is **ME**.
This old carnal nature must be brought under subjection to **YOU**.
I confess my sin of pride and the sin of "SEE ME."
Teach me to be humble and no matter what my calling might be,
Let me always joyfully <u>GIVE ALL THE CREDIT TO YOU!</u>

SLR ~

DEAR YOUNG MOTHERS TO BE

It might seem strange that we would greet you this way today. Well, let me tell you why.

Someday, Lord willing, you will become a mother but before that day comes, allow us to share a few facts with you. You are a very special person and God made no mistake when He made you. Of all the people in the world, there is no one else exactly like you.

YOU ARE SOMEBODY. YOU ARE NO JUNK. YOU ARE LOVED AND APPRECIATED BECAUSE YOU ARE WONDERFUL.

Because all this is true, you don't have to settle for junk. You don't have to allow anyone to put you down or to make you feel worthless and useless. That is why you don't have to follow this world's system that says, "If it feels good, do it." You don't have to allow your body to be used in the wrong way with loose sexual living and with body and mind destroying drugs.

After all, the children you will bear someday will need strong and healthy bodies and minds and you are the one who determines that. You are the one who can begin to prepare now but making some important decisions that only you can make.

We encourage you to do things God's way. You have the right to save your body until the man comes along that God wants to be your husband. After marriage, then the children can come. As we all know, that is not the popular way things are done today. But YOU CAN CHANGE THAT FOR YOUR LIFE.

Start now asking the Lord to be the head of your life. Ask Him to direct you to the right husband and then ask Him to make you a good wife and mother. One who will love her children, respect them and raise them according to God's standard.

Your children will be raised in a cruel world but God can help enable you to be both strength and protection for them. Have you heard the saying that, "THE HAND THAT ROCKS THE CRADLE, RULES THE WORLD?" That means that, as a Mother, YOU can help change the world by the way you raise the children that God will someday bless you and your husband to have.

So, young mother-to-be, you can start today to prepare yourself for that great day when you will be a loving mother and we will be able to say to you CONGRATULATIONS AND HAPPY MOTHER'S DAY.

SLR ~ ~ Mother's Day

IS IT TIME TO COME HOME?

(Our Sunday School lesson comes from St. John 17. When I got to verse 4, the Holy Spirit stopped me and led me to write this poem.)

Lord, is it time to come home?
  Has my work here been completed?
    Did I pass the exam of life?
      Or is there time for failed courses to be repeated?

Did I glorify you or did I lift up myself?
  Was "I" on display while "thou" was left on the shelf?
    The treasures I was entrusted with, did I squander
    Too much for myself?
      And did I leave for you only the crumbs that were left?

What about my loved ones?
  Did I release them unto thee?
    Or, with my limited knowledge,
      Did I attempt to untangle their lives and
      Make them just like me?

Lord, how many times did I falter?
  How many times did I fail?
    I have no idea of the number of times,
      But the exact count you know very well.

I'm thankful that I know you
  And that for me you died.
    You shed your blood on Calvary
      For me you were crucified.

You've prepared a place for me
  And now you're coming to take me home.
    All my faults and failures will be left behind.
      I'll never be left alone.

I can rejoice
 Throughout eternity.
  Not because I have been perfect
   But because you have set me free.

SLR ~

PLEASE, I'VE HAD ENOUGH SADNESS

You remind me of the deep dark pit from which I have come.

You remind me of the suffering the injustice bestowed upon me and mine.

You remind me of the hatred and the brutality I have suffered.

You remind me it was purposely done "by others."

Who wanted to enslave my body, my soul, my mind.

You remind me that I should be thankful
That you came to enlighten me.

You said your "revelation" would satisfy and set me free.

Knowledgeable One, allow me one question if you will.

With all you have told me, why am I in misery still?

Knowing the past is important but guidance for the future is what I need.

Don't fill my young mind with hatred from the past.
Please, I earnestly plead.

Please, I've had enough sadness
Please, try to bring me some joy.
Please, please bring me some joy,
You who pretend to be the Knowledgeable One.

Thank you, for leading me out of confusion
And giving me respect
Thank you, for helping me to hold my head erect.
Thank you, for reminding me that I am somebody.

Thank you, for reminding me that I have worth.
Thank you, for reminding me that I am special to you.

You light up my life! You put joy in my heart and guess what?
It makes me respect myself and others too.

You are a wonderful friend/husband/cousin/etc.

Still Searching,

Some Girl, Some Boy

SLR ~

AN OPEN LETTER TO JEANETTE

Hi Jeanette. This is Shirley.

So, you slipped away from us yesterday. You know that not only Tom, but all of us will miss you. The Laura addition will never be the same.

You and Tom were a bright light shining in our neighborhood. Your yard was the "Meeting Place" for many of us. It was calming, soothing and refreshing. You would offer us cokes, ice cream and even Italian dishes.

Remember when you told us that you and Tom would soon be celebrating your 50th anniversary? Jean, Sybil and I got together to plan a small surprise celebration for you. However, as word got out in the neighborhood, EVERYBODY wanted to play a part. Our "surprise" celebration was four times as large as we had expected. You and Tom were surprised and we had a ball.

How you loved to collect owls! During my travels, it was a pleasure to look for all types to bring back to you. You were so appreciative. Tom would tease you by saying, "Jeanette loves to receive gifts."

After Willie had heart surgery I was having difficulty getting him to change his eating habits. I remember the advice you gave as you looked him straight in the eye and said with that gravelly voice, "Well, if he won't do right, just beat the hell out of him." He laughed for a week. But, IT WORKED! Thank you for the good advice.

On occasion I had the privilege of talking with you and Tom about Jesus, the blessed Savior. Hopefully, you not only heard but heeded the message. If you did, there will be no need for me to say goodbye because I will see you again. So I'll just say I'll see you later ... on the other side of life.

SLR ~

SHE'S GONE HOME

Our Dear Mother has a new home
      And it's as fine as fine can be!
The Architect who designed it
      Made it a beauty for the eyes to see!

It doesn't have Texas weather
      No mosquitoes. No extreme cold or heat.
Her new home maintains the perfect temperature.
      Now, that's hard to beat!

Her years of serving Jesus
      Are being rewarded now
Her voice will no longer be heard at Christ Mission
      But in the Heavenly Angelic Choir.

Her working days are over.
      That is a thing of the past.
She will be taken care of throughout eternity
      And has security and benefits that will last ... and last.

No more doctors for Mama George to see,
      No more aches and no more pain!
She has a new body
      And will never suffer again.

Mother, you made the right decision
      Many years ago.
You took Jesus as your Savior
      And your love for Him did show.

SHOUT ON NOW IN GLORY!
      YOU HAVE RECEIVED YOUR REWARD!
We'll see you one day in Glory
      When we, too, from this life depart.

UNTIL THEN ...... FAREWELL, MOTHER.

SLR ~

IN HONOR OF ETHEL

26 years is a long time
To struggle for the Lord
Realism causes us to admit it isn't always easy
In fact, sometimes it's very hard.

Yet the joys outweigh the sorrows
Because service has been unto the Lord
What rejoicing Double Rock has seen
When we have been on one accord.

To you friends and members
To the saints and sinners too
We extend a heartfelt welcome
Because Jesus also loves you!

Please come again.

[This was written for Ethel Dennis, the wife of my cousin Allen Dennis. She served as an usher at Double Rock Missionary Baptist Church in Compton, California. She and others were being honored during an afternoon service. She asked me to write a poem for her and this was it.]

THE CHRIST CHILD IN AFRICA

BY AUNT MARGARET TRAUB
(Poet - Liberia)

Aunt Margaret Traub was a gifted writer, and a confident person with a heart full of love for everyone. Writing was her passion. She was an active member of our Missionary Women's Fellowship and would encourage each of us to write a poem or something about our experiences. She then compiled these in a booklet and presented one to each of us. She wrote many wonderful poems but this is one of my favorites. Perhaps one day her family will decide to publish some of her writings.

God sent His Son to Africa
When Herod tried to kill the child
This continent men once called "dark,"
God chose as refuge for the Christ

'Twas on this land the little Boy
Took His first faltering steps
'Twas here among us Africans
His consciousness of love began;
How great is God!
His wisdom and His love,
How deep and wide!

We see tall, dark-skinned mothers
With babies on their backs,
Of eggs or rice, or market stuff
To show "good heart"
For Mary and her family;
We see their merry children
With lovely Child of God
Delighting in His laugh,

Surrounding Him with love and care;
(One day an African
Would help Him with His cross.)

Let Gladness spread o're Africa!
Let songs and dance express our Joy
For God in graciousness and love
Gave us full share in Christ, His Son!

Bringing small gifts
Playing in the yard.

EBOLA

An Enemy is stalking the land as it unmercifully claims lives ... By the hundreds ... By the thousands ... And possibly by the millions ... if it is not stopped.

Entire communities are being destroyed:
- Families are losing several members <u>in one day</u>
- With few treatment centers available, men, women and children, are dying by the side of roads, under trees or wherever this Enemy stalks them
- Life is filled with fear because a simple handshake can cause death
- Schools are closed
- Government buildings are closed
- Businesses are closed
- There are shortages of food and decent drinking water.

Wait! Let me stop writing about all of this!
Many of us have wept, we have questioned "Why", and we have prayed many prayers.

"Is there no balm (medicine) in Gilead? Is there no physician there? Why is there no healing for the wounds of my people?"

"If only my head were a pool of water
And my eyes a fountain of tears,
I would weep day and night
for all my people who have been slaughtered."
        Jeremiah 8:22 and 9:1 (NLT)

Let's pray to THE GOD WHO ANSWERS PRAYER. He alone, is able to defeat this dreaded enemy called <u>EBOLA</u>.

As we turn to Him who has ALL POWER, Let's "Cast ALL of our cares upon Him because He cares for us."

SLR ~

COMING SOON

GO TO AFRICA? WHO? NOT ME!!!!

The Memoirs of a Missionary

By Shirley Dennis Richards

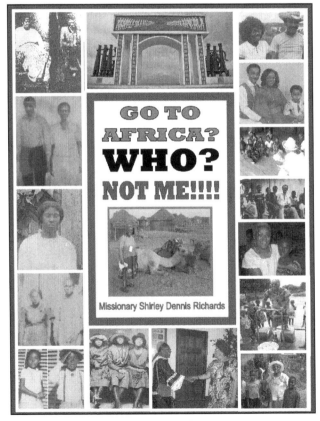

CONTACT:

whobby980@aol.com

To God be the glory!!

Missionary Shirley L. Dennis Richards